Fishing Wit

FISHING WIT

Summersdale Publishers Ltd
46 West Street
Chichester
West Sussex
PO19 1RP
UK

www.summersdale.com

Printed and bound by CPI Group (UK) Ltd, Croydon, CR0 4YY

ISBN: 978-1-84953-187-0

Substantial discounts on bulk quantities of Summersdale books are available to corporations, professional associations and other organisations. For details contact Summersdale Publishers by telephone: +44 (0) 1243 771107, fax: +44 (0) 1243 786300 or email: nicky@summersdale.com.

Fishing Wit

Quips and Quotes for the Avid Angler

Richard Benson

Illustrations by Ian Baker

summersdale

To MICHAEL
HAPPY 80TH
BIRTHDAY
Mike X

Contents

Editor's Note

For centuries, man has been finding solace at the edge of rivers, lakes and ponds, whiling away the hours in the pursuit of that elusive creature: the fish. As Roderick Haig-Brown attests, 'Our tradition is that of the first man who sneaked away to the creek when the tribe did not really need fish.' Whether it is for solitude, camaraderie, the desire to be with nature or actually for need of food, men and women have always looked for excuses to go a-fishing; although the actual catching of fish may feature less often than one would like.

Whether a fisherman, an angler, or simply a cod-and-chips kind of person, it seems everyone has something to say about the noble sport of fishing – some of them are even truthful; which can't always be said for this breed of man (or woman!). Whether debating the fisherman's questionable attire or proclaiming their love of all things fishy, this book is full of the wittiest and best quotations and is sure to leave you reeling.

FISHING 101

All you need to
be a fisherman is
patience and a worm.

Herb Shriner

Most of the world is covered by water. A fisherman's job is simple: pick out the best parts.

Charles Waterman

Work: a dangerous disorder affecting high public functionaries who want to go fishing.

Ambrose Bierce

Fish, I love you and respect you very much. But I will kill you dead before this day ends.

Ernest Hemingway, *The Old Man and the Sea*

I fish better with a lit cigar; some people fish better with talent.

Nick Lyons

Angling is extremely time-consuming. That's sort of the whole point.

Thomas McGuane

Carpe Diem does
not mean 'Fish
of the Day'.

Anonymous

Line: something you give your
co-workers when they ask
on Monday how your fishing
went the past weekend.

Anonymous

Good fishing is a matter of timing.
You have to get there yesterday.

Milton Berle

Fishing, if I a fisher may protest,
Of pleasures is the sweetest
of sports, the best
Of exercises the most excellent
Of recreations the most innocent.
But now the sport is marred,
and why you ask?
Fishes decrease, and fishers multiply.

Thomas Bastard, *Chrestoleros*

Soon after I embraced the sport
of angling I became convinced
that I should never be able to
enjoy it if I had to rely on the
cooperation of the fish.

Sparse Grey Hackle

If the shattered globe were falling
to pieces about his ears [the
angler] would be found hurrying
off to his favorite stream, rod
in hand, that he might perish
there decently and in order.

H. T. Sheringham, *An Angler's Hours*

A rod: an attractively painted length
of fibreglass that keeps an angler
from ever getting too close to a fish.

Anonymous

THE ONE THAT
GOT AWAY

My best fishing
memory is about
some fish that I
never caught.

George Orwell

Oh give me grace to catch a fish
So big that even I
When talking of it afterwards
Have no need to lie

Anonymous

I never lost a little fish –
yes, I'm free to say.
It always was the biggest fish
I caught, that got away.

Eugene Field

Fishing largely consists of
not catching fish; failure is as
much a part of the sport as
knee injuries are of football.

Robert Hughes

I have fished through
fishless days that I remember
happily without regret.

Roderick Haig-Brown

A sly old fish, too cunning
for the hook.

George Crabbe

There's a reason they call it
'fishing' and not 'catching'.

Anonymous

It has always been
my private conviction
that any man who
pits his intelligence
against a fish and
loses, has it coming.

John Steinbeck

GIVE A MAN A FISH

Give a man a fish
and you feed him for
a day. Teach a man
to fish and he will
bore you stupid.

Lorrie B. Potters

Catch a man a fish, and you
can sell it to him. Teach a man
to fish and you ruin a wonderful
business opportunity.

Karl Marx

If you teach a man to fish, you'll
never sell your fish at the market.

Cheryl A. Soper

Give a man a fish and he'll feast for a day. Give him a fishing rod and chances are he'll starve.

Anonymous

Give a man a fish and he eats for a day. Teach him to fish and you get rid of him for the entire weekend.

Zenna Schaffer

Give a man a fish, and he can eat
for a day. But teach a man how to
fish, and he'll be dead of mercury
poisoning inside of three years.

Charles Haas

Teach a man to fish and you
feed him for a lifetime. Unless
he doesn't like sushi – then you
also have to teach him to cook.

Auren Hoffman

Give a man a fish
and you'll feed him
for a day. Teach a
man to fish and he'll
buy a funny hat.

Scott Adams

LEAKY RELATIONSHIPS

Fishing? That was always your bloody problem! Fishing outside off stump!

Geoffrey Boycott to David 'Bumble' Lloyd

Wanted: Good woman who can cook, sew, clean fish, has boat and motor. Send photo of boat and motor.

Old fishing sign

An angler is a man who spends rainy days sitting around on the muddy banks of rivers doing nothing because his wife won't let him do it at home.

Anonymous

Your first trout is like your first love. You never forget it!

Jimmy D. Moore

In fly fishing, compromises are often perfectly acceptable; there are few absolutes... You could say the same thing about marriage.

Ken Marsh

❦

Somebody just back of you while you are fishing is as bad as someone looking over your shoulder while you write a letter to your girl.

Ernest Hemingway

❦

The best way to a fisherman's heart is through his fly.

Anonymous

She is such a good friend that she
would throw all her acquaintances
into the water for the pleasure
of fishing them out again.

Charles Maurice de Talleyrand

Despite all the variables and advice,
like love and marriage it seemed
to me that learning to cast ought
to be a lot easier than it was.

Jessica Maxwell

Some men
would rather be
photographed
with their fish than
with their wives.

Gwen Cooper and Evelyn Haas,
Wade a Little Deeper, Dear

Fishing is such great fun, I
have often felt, that it really
ought to be done in bed.

Robert Traver

When you fish for love, bait with
your heart, not your brain.

Mark Twain

LOOKING FLY

Then there's wet-weather gear, a good pair of waders... mind you, that's just 'cause I love dressing up in rubber.

Chris Tarrant

I've always tied my own flies. I
started with puce-pink feathers
from Bonnie Langford's boa.

Bernard Cribbins

—◆—

There is no taking trout
in dry breeches.

Miguel de Cervantes

—◆—

Only a fisherman thinks it's
worth spending one hundred
dollars for a fishing outfit to
catch one dollar's worth of fish.

Anonymous

Why do they call them waders?
They don't wade. Why not call them
leakers? That's what they do best.

Randal Sumner

No shoes, no shirt... no problem.

Sign in a fishing club in the Bahamas

I don't think there is anything sexier than just standing in waders with a fly rod. I just love it.

Linda Hamilton

Its battered crown and well-frayed band, preserves not only the memory of every trout he caught, but also the smell.

Corey Ford on the importance of a fisherman's hat

Fishing costs like sin but requires heavier clothing.

L. C. Clower

CAUGHT CUISINE

They say fish should swim thrice... first it should swim in the sea, then it should swim in butter, and at last, sirrah, it should swim in good claret.

Jonathan Swift

I'm on a seafood diet. I
see food and I eat it.

Les Dawson

———

Why does Sea World have
a seafood restaurant? I could
be eating a slow learner.

Lynda Montgomery

———

A trout in the pot is better
than a salmon in the sea.

Irish proverb

Oh, no doubt the cod is a splendid swimmer – admirable for swimming purposes but not for eating.

Oscar Wilde

If it swims, it's edible.

Bill Demmond

Smoked carp tastes just as good as smoked salmon when you ain't got no smoked salmon.

Patrick F. McManus

Mere wishes for fishes
aren't edible dishes.

Julian Snow

———◆———

Sometimes I do like a couple of
cooperative fish of frying size.

John Steinbeck

———◆———

Fly fishing is no good for
vegetarians, but is just about perfect
for contemplative carnivores.

Anonymous

Oysters are the most tender and delicate of all seafoods. They stay in bed all day and night.

Hector Bolitho

I never drink water because of the disgusting things that fish do in it.

W. C. Fields

You know why fish are so thin? They eat fish.

Jerry Seinfeld

I'd pose naked for a million pounds
– but I wouldn't eat a live fish.

Nicky Byrne

———•———

Soup and fish explain half
the emotions of human life.

Sydney Smith

———•———

Fish should smell like the tide. Once
they smell like fish, it's too late.

Oscar Gizelt

Shellfish are the prime cause of the decline of morals and the adaptation of an extravagant lifestyle.

Pliny the Elder

In Mexico we have a word for sushi: bait.

Jose Simon

PLENTY MORE
FISH IN THE SEA

Oceans are getting
so polluted that the
other day I caught
a tuna fish that was
already packed in oil.

Charlie Viracola

The fishermen know that the sea is dangerous and the storm is terrible, but they have never found these dangers sufficient reason for remaining ashore.

Vincent van Gogh

───•───

The sea hath fish for every man.

William Camden

───•───

There are fish in the sea better than have ever been caught.

Irish proverb

Saltwater fishing is only for the strong man with a hard stomach. It's like sex after lunch.

Charles Ritz

I mean, here I am, one small guy with a fishing rod, on this vast sea, and out there in the vast expanse of the ocean are these hundreds of millions of fish... laughing at me.

Anonymous

There is indeed, perhaps, no better
way to hold communion with the
sea than sitting in the sun on the
veranda of a fishermen's cafe.

Joseph W. Beach

Ocean: a body of water occupying
two-thirds of a world made
for man – who has no gills.

Ambrose Bierce

No good fish goes
anywhere without
a porpoise.

Lewis Carroll

The sea has never been friendly
to man. At most it has been the
accomplice of human restlessness.

Joseph Conrad

I don't know who named them
'swells'. There's nothing swell
about them. They should
have named them 'awfuls'.

Hugo Vihlen

SPINNING THE YARN

Of all the liars
among mankind,
the fisherman is the
most trustworthy.

William Sherwood Fox

Nothing makes a fish bigger
than almost being caught.

Anonymous

All fishermen are liars; it's an
occupational disease with them, like
housemaid's knee or editor's ulcers.

Beatrice Cook

Do not tell fish stories where
the people know you; but
particularly, don't tell them
where they know the fish.

Mark Twain

Fishermen are born honest,
but they get over it.

Ed Zern

❦

Fishing is a delusion entirely
surrounded by liars in old clothes.

Don Marquis

❦

For at least the last 275 years
the honesty of fishermen has
been somewhat questionable.

Arthur Ransome

Even eminent chartered accountants are known, in their capacity as fishermen, blissfully to ignore differences between seven and ten inches, half a pound and two pounds, three fish and a dozen fish.

William Sherwood Fox

Whether catch and release or not, the fish keep growing long after they've been caught.

Ian Mitchell

Arkansas fishing rules: bait your own hook; clean your own fish; tell your own lies.

Jimmy D. Moore

There are some achievements which are never done in the presence of those who hear of them. Catching salmon is one, and working all night is another.

Anthony Trollope

Early to bed, early to rise;
fish all day, make up lies.

Anonymous

Mere bald fabrication is useless;
the veriest tyro can manage that.
It is in the circumstantial detail, the
embellishing touches of probability,
the general air of scrupulous –
almost of pedantic – veracity, that
the experienced angler is seen.

Jerome K. Jerome

FLY GUYS

Fly fishing is like sex, everyone thinks there is more than there is, and that everyone is getting more than their share.

Henry Kanemoto

Fly fishers are usually brain-workers in society.

James A. Henshall

I fell in love with a fly fisherman...
I can't believe my competition
is fish, and not other women.

Allison Moir

Fly fishing is the most fun
you can have standing up.

Arnold Gingrich

To paraphrase a deceased
patriot, I regret I have only one
life to give to my fly fishing.

Robert Traver

Never, with a fly rod
in my hand have I
been less than in a
place that was less
than beautiful.

Charles Kuralt

Whether I caught fish or not,
just the thrill of rolling out that
line and watching my fly turn over
has been good enough for me.

Curt Gowdy

———◆———

The difference between fly
fishers and worm dunkers is
the quality of their excuses.

Anonymous

BE QUIET AND
GO A-ANGLING

Angling may be said
to be so like the
mathematics that it can
never be fully learnt.

Izaak Walton

Angling is an amusement peculiarly adapted to the mild and cultivated scenery of England.

Washington Irving

———

It is sufficient to know that the art of angling requires as much enthusiasm as poetry... as much caution as housebreaking.

Genio Scott

———

[They] make gentle and inoffensive creatures sound like wounded buffalo and man-eating tigers.

Roderick Haig-Brown on anglers

Anglers have a way of romanticising
their battles with fish.

Ernest Hemingway

It is to be observed that 'angling'
is the name given to fishing
by people who can't fish.

Stephen Leacock

An angler, sir, uses the finest tackle,
and catches his fish scientifically –
trout for instance – with the artificial
fly, and he is mostly a quiet, well-
behaved gentleman. A fisherman,
sir, uses any kind of 'ooks and
lines, and catches them any way;
so how he gets them it's all one
to 'im, and he is generally a noisy
fellah, sir, something like a gunner.

Dr George Washington Bethune

The music of angling is
more compelling to me than
anything contrived in the
greatest symphony hall.

A. J. McLane

FISHY BUSINESS

If fishing is interfering
with your business,
give up your business.

Sparse Grey Hackle

The only reason I ever played golf in the first place was so I could afford to hunt and fish.

Sam Snead

As for lawyers, they are an incorrigible race. Indeed, I have rarely seen any of them who can angle at all, perhaps only one: and he was a sinister biped.

James O'Gorman

There are only two occasions when Americans respect privacy, especially in Presidents. Those are praying and fishing.

Herbert Hoover

A countryman between two lawyers
is like a fish between two cats.

Benjamin Franklin

If all politicians fished instead
of spoke publicly, we would
be at peace with the world.

Will Rogers

I only make movies to
finance my fishing.

Lee Marvin

I used to take
worms on tour.

Adrian Smith of Iron Maiden

In cross-examination,
as in fishing, nothing is
more ungainly than a
fisherman pulled into
the water by his catch.

Louis Nizer

HOT SPOTS

There is no use in
your walking five miles
to fish when you can
depend on being
just as unsuccessful
near home.

Mark Twain

Wherever the fish are,
that's where we go.

Richard Wagner

❧

It's a pretty good rule never to show
a favourite spot to any fisherman
you wouldn't trust with your wife.

Robert Traver

❧

Never doubt the environmental
knowledge of a consistently
successful fisherman. Always
doubt the motives of a
consistently argumentative
environmental bureaucrat.

Jim Slinsky

Good roads lead to bad fishing.

Eric Wight

I really fished mainly because
I wanted to be alone on
the middle of a lake.

Susan A. Toth

Fish say, they have their
stream and pond;
But is there anything beyond?

Rupert Brooke, from 'Heaven'

The mark of a successful man
is one that has spent an entire
day on the bank of a river
without feeling guilty about it.

Chinese proverb

And this, our life, exempt
from public haunt,
Finds tongues in trees, books
in the running brooks,
Sermons in stones, and
good in every thing.

William Shakespeare, *As You Like It*

Best fishing in troubled waters.

Sir John Harrington

A RIVER RUNS
THROUGH IT

We have sat on the
river bank and caught
catfish with pin hooks.
The time has come
to harpoon a whale.

John Hope

Here, on the river's verge, I could
be busy for months without
changing my place, simply leaning
a little more to right or left.

Paul Cézanne

He who postpones the hour of living
is like the rustic who waits for the
river to run out before he crosses.

Horace

The traveller fancies he has seen the country. So he has, the outside of it at least; but the angler only sees the inside. The angler only is brought close, face to face with the flower and bird and insect life of the rich river banks, the only part of the landscape where the hand of man has never interfered.

Charles Kingsley

A river is the cosiest
of friends. You
must love it and
live with it before
you can know it.

G. W. Curtis

When you are on the river, ocean
or in the woods, you are the closest
to the truth you'll ever get.

Jack Leonard

❧

The angler forgets most of the
fish he catches, but he does not
forget the streams and lakes
in which they are caught.

Charles K. Fox

GONE FISHIN'

I prefer any kind
of fishing to any
kind of work.

Ed Zern

Our tradition is that of the first man
who sneaked away to the creek when
the tribe did not really need fish.

Roderick Haig-Brown

You can't say enough about fishing.
Though the sport of kings, it's
just what the deadbeat ordered.

Thomas McGuane

I spend most of my life fishing,
the rest I just waste.

Anonymous

The two best times to go fishing?
When it is raining and when it is not.

Patrick F. McManus

By common consent fishing is
the most peaceful of all forms of
sport, exception might perhaps
be made of snail-hunting in
a well-ordered garden.

H. T. Sheringham

I like to shoot fish in a barrel.
But I like to do it after the
water has run out.

Warren Buffett

Fishing seems to
be the favourite
form of loafing.

Edgar Watson Howe

BOAT QUOTES

There is nothing,
absolutely nothing,
half so much
worth doing as
simply messing
about in boats.

Kenneth Grahame, *The Wind in the Willows*

There are a lot of mysterious things about boats, such as why anyone would get on one voluntarily.

P. J. O'Rourke, *Holidays in Hell*

❦

Wherever you take your boat, make sure your brain arrives five minutes earlier.

Sailor's proverb

❦

A fisherman's walk: three steps and overboard.

Marcus Valerius Martialis

No one likes an ugly boat,
however cheap or fast.

Roger Duncan

❦

Fortune brings in some boats
that are not steered.

William Shakespeare, *Cymbeline*

❦

Nodding the head does
not row the boat.

Irish proverb

Boats, like whisky,
are all good.

R. D. 'Pete' Culler

Let your boat of life be light,
packed with only what you need.

Jerome K. Jerome, *Three Men in a Boat*

If a man is to be obsessed by
something, I suppose a boat is
as good as anything, perhaps
a bit better than most.

E. B. White

THE END OF THE LINE

When you bait the
hook with your heart,
the fish always bite.

John Burroughs

There is no greater fan of
fly fishing than the worm.

Patrick F. McManus

Good things come to those who bait.

Anonymous

He catches the best fish who
angles with a golden hook.

Latin proverb

Fly fishing may be a sport invented
by insects with fly fishermen as bait.

P. J. O'Rourke

If I'm not going to catch
anything, then I'd rather not
catch anything on flies.

Bob Lawless

You never see a fish on the
wall with its mouth shut.

Sally Berger

—◆—

You must lose a fly to catch a trout.

George Herbert

Chance is always powerful.
Let your hook be always cast;
in the pool where you least
expect it, there will be a fish.

Ovid

❦

A man may fish with the worm that
hath eat of a king, and eat of the
fish that hath fed of that worm.

William Shakespeare, *Hamlet*

All fish are not caught with flies.

John Lyly

If you fish the wrong fly long
and hard enough, it will sooner
or later become the right fly.

John Gierach

Bait: a preparation that renders
the hook more palatable.
The best kind is beauty.   ·

Ambrose Bierce

The profound difference
that divides the human race is
a question of bait – whether
to fish with worms or not.

Virginia Woolf

CATCH OF THE DAY

The fishing was good;
it was the catching
that was bad.

A. K. Best

If I fished only to capture fish, my fishing trips would have ended long ago.

Zane Grey

He was a little happy. But also a little, 'Hmm. I teach her fishing and SHE gets the record.'

Pam Marvin, on husband Lee Marvin's reaction when she caught a world-record blue marlin

Bragging may not
bring happiness,
but no man that ever
caught a large amount
of fish goes home
through an alley.

Ann Landers

Even if you've been fishing for three
hours and haven't caught anything
except poison ivy and sunburn,
you're still better off than the worm.

Anonymous

A fisherman is always hopeful
– nearly always more hopeful
than he has any right to be.

Roderick Haig-Brown

This planet is covered with sordid men who demand that he who spends time fishing shall show returns in fish.

Leonidas Hubbard Jr

For the supreme test of a fisherman is... what he has caught when he has caught no fish.

John H. Bradley

Fishing consists of a series of
misadventures interspersed by
occasional moments of glory.

Howard Marshall

Game fish are too valuable
to only be caught once.

Lee Wulff

At once Victorious, with
your hands and eyes,
You make the fishes and
the Men your prize,
And while the pleasing
Slavery we Court,
I fear you captivate us
both for Sport.

**Attached to the eighteenth-century
print,** *The Angelic Angler*

If you want to catch more
fish, use more hooks.

George Allen Sr

You must always let your hook be
hanging. When you least expect
it, a great fish will swim by.

Og Mandino

—◆—

Now, happy fisherman;
now twitch the line!
How thy rod bends! behold,
the prize is thine!

John Gay, from 'Rural Sports'

For angling rod he took
a sturdy oake;
For line, a cable that in
storm ne'er broke;
His hooke was such as
heads the end of pole;
To pluck down house ere
fire consumes it whole;
The hooke was baited
with a dragon's tail;
And then on rock he stood
to bob for whale.

William Davenant, *Britannia Triumphans*

TIME SCALES

The gods do not deduct from man's allotted span the hours spent in fishing.

Babylonian proverb

To tell the truth, fishermen remain always boys as far as their amusement goes.

Harold Russell

Man does not cease to fish because he gets old, Man gets old because he ceases to fish!

Anonymous

Time flies so fast after youth is past that we cannot accomplish one half of the many things we have in mind or indeed one half our duties. The only safe and sensible plan is to make other things give way to the essentials, and the first of these is fly fishing.

Theodore Gordon

Fishing yesterday. Fishing today.
Fishing tomorrow. I must be retired.

Anonymous

If people concentrated on the really
important things of life, there'd
be a shortage of fishing rods.

Doug Larson

Many men go fishing all their
lives without knowing it is
not fish they are after.

Henry David Thoreau

It is the glory of the art of angling
that its disciples never grow old.
The muscles may relax and the
beloved rod become a burden,
but the fire of enthusiasm kindled
in youth is never extinguished.

George Dawson, *Pleasures of Angling with
Rod and Reel for Trout and Salmon*

Telling a teenager the facts of life is like giving a fish a bath.

Arnold H. Glasow

❦

You don't meet many five-year-olds who are not interested in a hedgehog or a stickleback.

David Attenborough

❦

I just think it's fantastic to see old people going fishing with young people and teaching them things.

Rex Hunt

WHAT LIES BENEATH

The books all say that barracuda rarely eat people, but very few barracuda can read.

Dave Barry

Our plenteous streams a
various race supply,
The bright-eyed perch with
fins of Tyrian dye,
The silver eel, in shining
volumes roll'd,
The yellow carp, in scales
bedropp'd with gold,
Swift trouts, diversified
with crimson stains,
And pikes, the tyrants
of the wat'ry plains.

Alexander Pope, from 'Windsor Forest'

You won't find one fish in a million that has enough sense to come in when it rains.

Robert Benchley

Here comes the trout that must be caught with tickling.

William Shakespeare, *Twelfth Night*

Enjoy thy stream, O harmless Fish!
And when an Angler, for his dish,
Through gluttony's vile sin,
Attempts, a wretch, to pull the out;
God give thee strength,
O gentle Trout,
To pull the raskall in!

John Wolcott, from 'To a Fish of the Brook'

The salmon is the
most stately fish that
any man may angle
to in fresh water.

Juliana Barnes

A steelhead always knows where
he is going, but a man seldom does.

Steve Raymond

If today were a fish I'd throw it back.

Anonymous

When you feel neglected, think
of the female salmon, who lays
three million eggs but no one
remembers her on Mother's Day.

Sam Ewing

If you want to catch a trout,
don't fish in a herring barrel.

Ann Landers

A chub is the worst fish that swims.

Izaak Walton

I believe that lobsters
are the result of
a terrible genetic
accident involving
nuclear radiation
and cockroaches.

Dave Barry

THE DOWNSIDE

Fishing is fundamentally a game of chance, and at heart we are all gamblers.

Dorothy Noyes Arms

In literature, fishing is indeed
an exhilarating sport; but... it
does not pan out when you
carry the idea further.

Irvin S. Cobb

There is a fine line between
fishing and just standing on
the shore like an idiot.

Steven Wright

Ladies, when you are fly fishing,
and nature calls, life is not fair.

Anonymous

————•————

Fish and visitors smell in three days.

Benjamin Franklin

My mere presence has spoiled
the fishing in half a dozen states.

Art Scheck

And it is discipline in the equality of
men, for all men are equal before fish.

Herbert Hoover

As a rule, men are very
forgiving when you fish badly.
It's only when you fish well
that they get truly upset.

Mallory Burton

Fish is the only food that
is considered spoiled once
it smells like what it is.

P. J. O'Rourke

Believe me, a group of fishermen
walking up the towpath is worse
than the army on manoeuvres.

Steve Haywood

SOMETHING TO POND-ER

When I was feeling
good, I'd have dreams
full of giant pike
that were perhaps
also leopards.

Ted Hughes

Time is but the stream
I go a-fishing in.

Henry David Thoreau

———

Govern a family as you would
cook a small fish – very gently.

Chinese proverb

No gulls, no luck.

French proverb

Fish are strange creatures. They're
even more unpredictable than
women – and that's going some.

R. V. 'Gadabout' Gaddis

The only certainty in fishing
is that there is no certainty.

Eric Horsfall

[Writing is] like salmon fishing. It's so hard to catch a book in the nets of time.

Sebastian Barry

❦

Men can learn a lot from fishing – when the fish are biting there is no problem in the world big enough to be remembered.

Orlando A. Battista

They may the better fish in the
water when it is troubled.

Richard Grafton

The fish in the water is silent,
the animal on the earth is noisy,
the bird in the air is singing.
But man has in him
the silence of the sea, the
noise of the earth
and the music of the air.

Rabindranath Tagore, from 'Stray Birds'

The charm of fishing is that it
is the pursuit of what is elusive
but attainable, a perpetual
series of occasions for hope.

John Buchan

I go fishing not to find myself
but to lose myself.

Joseph Monninger

The finest gift you can give to
any fisherman is to put a good
fish back, and who knows if
the fish that you caught isn't
someone else's gift to you?

Lee Wulff

I think fish is nice, but then I think
that rain is wet, so who am I to judge?

**Douglas Adams, *The Restaurant
at the End of the Universe***

Be patient and calm – for no
one can catch fish in anger.

Herbert Hoover

ANGLERS KNOW BEST

If you want to be happy for a day, get drunk... If you want to be happy for life, go fishing.

Nigel Botherway

The greatest losses an angler
can sustain are those of his
patience and good temper; they
are worth a cartload of salmon.

Thomas Tod Stoddard

Listen to the sound of the river
and you will get a trout.

Irish proverb

Never test the depth of the
water with both feet.

Anonymous

There is only one theory about
angling in which I have perfect
confidence, and this is that the
two words, least appropriate to
any statement, about it, are the
words 'always' and 'never'.

Lord Edward Grey

The best day to go fishing is
any day that ends in a 'Y'.

George Carr

⚫──◆──⚫

You can learn more from a
guide in one day than you can
in three months fishing alone.

Mario López

There ain't but one time to go fishin', and that's whenever you can.

Diron Talbert

I believe the solution to any problem – work, love, money, whatever – is to go fishing, and the worse the problem, the longer the trip should be.

John Gierach

Fishing is not an escape from life, but often a deeper immersion into it.

Harry Middleton

ONE STICKLEBACK
SHORT OF A SHOAL

Fishermen, like the
rest of humankind,
will talk relentlessly
and authoritatively
about what they
understand least.

Ted Leeson

Fishing is a jerk on one end
of the line waiting for a jerk on
the other end of the line.

Mark Twain

The fish and I were both
stunned and disbelieving to find
ourselves connected by a line.

William Humphrey

There never was an angler who lived
but that there was a fish capable
of taking the conceit out of him.

Zane Grey

There never was an angler who lived

I know that the human being and
the fish can coexist peacefully.

George W. Bush

151

Fishing is
unquestionably a
form of madness, but
happily, for the once
bitten, there is no cure.

Lord Hume

Only an extraordinary person would purposely risk being outsmarted by a creature often less than twelve inches long, over and over again.

Anonymous

Creeps and idiots cannot conceal themselves for long on a fishing trip.

John Gierach

Men and fish wouldn't get
into trouble if they kept
their mouths shut.

Jimmy D. Moore

There he stands, draped in more
equipment than a telephone lineman,
trying to outwit an organism with a
brain no bigger than a breadcrumb,
and getting licked in the process.

Paul O'Neil

If there were no such thing
as optimism, there would be
no such thing as fishing.

Michael McIntosh

[Spending] serious money and
endless time to catch fish you
mostly release would by most
measures prove craziness.

James R. Babb

Fishing is the sport of
drowning worms.

Anonymous

[He] was fond of angling and was
apparently proud of being fond
of such a stupid occupation.

Leo Tolstoy, *Anna Karenina*

HOPE, FAITH
AND CATFISH

I love fishing. It's
transcendental
meditation with
a punchline.

Billy Connolly

When it comes to cults, fly fishing
isn't much different than most.

Ed Engle

Everyone ought to believe in
something; I believe I'll go fishing.

Anonymous

Blessings upon all that hate
contention, and love quietness,
and virtue, and Angling.

Izaak Walton

Throw a lucky man in the sea, and he
will come up with a fish in his mouth.

Arab proverb

Fishing is something between
a sport and a religion.

Josephine Tey

If fishing is a religion, fly
fishing is high church.

Tom Brokaw

Since three-fourths of the Earth's
surface is water, and one-fourth
is land, it is quite clear that the
good Lord intended us to spend
triple the amount of time fishing
as taking care of the lawn.

Chuck Clark

God is good but never
dance in a small boat.

Irish proverb

Some men go to church and
think about fishing, others go
fishing and think about God.

Tony Blake

Any kind of fishing provides
that connection with the
whole living world.

Ted Hughes

When a man picks up a fly rod
for the first time, he may not
know, he has been born again.

Joseph D. Farris

In my family, there was no clear division between religion and fly fishing.

Norman Maclean, *A River Runs Through It*

THE BENEFIT OF
THE TROUT

A trout is a moment
of beauty known only
to those who seek it.

Arnold Gingrich

All the romance of trout fishing
exists in the mind of the angler and
is in no way shared by the fish.

Harold F. Blaisdell, *The Philosophical Fisherman*

Has it ever struck you that trout
bite best on the Sabbath? God's
critters tempting decent men.

James Barrie

A trout fisherman is something
that defieth understanding.

Corey Ford

A trout stream for the initial cast?

What are more delightful than
one's emotions when approaching
a trout stream for the initial cast?

Nash Buckingham

Trout are like dreams hovering
in the elusive unconscious.

Kitty Pearson-Vincent

On the Firehole
I caught thirty-six
inches worth of trout
– in six instalments.

Arnold Gingrich

These brook trout will strike any
fly you present, provided you don't
get close enough to present it.

Dick Blalock

I salute the gallantry and
uncompromising standards of wild
trout, and their tastes in landscapes.

John Madson

Here lies Tommy Montague,
Whose love for Angling daily grew,
He died regretted, while late out,
To make a capture of a trout.

Epitaph

Successful trout fishing isn't
a matter of brute force or even
persistence, but something
more like infiltration.

John Gierach

Most anglers spend their lives in
making rules for trout, and trout
spend theirs in breaking them.

George Aston

If the trout be
the gentlemen of
the streams, then
the grayling is
certainly the lady!

Francis Francis

NICE TACKLE

Last year I went fishing with Salvador Dali. He was using a dotted line. He caught every other fish.

Steven Wright

The Essentials of
a Good Fly-Hook:
The temper of an
angel and penetration
of a prophet; fine
enough to be invisible
and strong enough
to kill a bull in a
ten-acre field.

G. S. Marryat

Most fishermen use the
double haul to throw their
casting mistakes further.

Lefty Kreh

A hook's well lost to catch a salmon.

French proverb

You Yourself are the water,
You Yourself are the fish,
and You Yourself are the net.
You Yourself cast the net, and
You Yourself are the bait.

Sri Guru Granth Sahib

I see the devil's hook and yet
can't help nibbling at his bait.

Moses Adams

Do not bite at the bait of
pleasure, till you know there
is no hook beneath it.

Thomas Jefferson

I have preached against indulgence,
but in truth I am a sentimental moron
when it comes to fishing tackle.

Harold F. Blaisdell, *The Philosophical Fisherman*

The man who coined
the phrase 'money
can't buy happiness'
never bought himself
a good fly rod!

Reg Baird

LIFE OR DEATH
FISHERMEN

There are worse
things in life than
death. Have you
ever spent an evening
with a fisherman?

Woody Allen

Bury me with my fly rod and my streamside kit so I can fish as I go down the River Styx.

Jimmy D. Moore

There's nothing to stop them
wearing rubber fishing gear
if they want, but that's really
bad for our emissions.

Allistair Anderson, senior crematorium officer

The trout do not rise in the
cemetery, so you better do your
fishing while you are still able.

Sparse Grey Hackle

My biggest worry is that my wife (when I'm dead) will sell my fishing gear for what I said I paid for it.

Koos Brandt

Jim is dead. Fishing boat for sale.

A fisherman's obituary

GOOD SPORT

Dorking Angling
Society – the
Manchester United
of the fishing world.

Jimmy Bullard

Catch-and-release fishing is a lot
like golf. You don't have to eat
the ball to have a good time.

Anonymous

Reading about baseball is a lot
more interesting than reading about
chess but you have to wonder: Don't
any of these guys ever go fishing?

Dave Shiflett

Fishing tournaments
seem a little like
playing tennis
with living balls.

Jim Harrison, *Just Before Dark*

[The] difference between big-game
fishing and weightlifting is that
weightlifters never clutter up their
library walls with stuffed barbells.

Ed Zern

I am not against golf, since I cannot
but suspect it keeps armies of the
unworthy from discovering trout.

Paul O'Neil

Fishing is the new golf
for footballers.

Phil Jagielka

Fishing is not like billiards, in
which it is possible to attain
a disgusting perfection.

Arthur Ransome

I fish, therefore
I don't golf.

Billy Connolly

THE ART OF SITTING

There is certainly
something in angling
that tends to produce
a serenity of the mind.

Washington Irving

Fish are, of course, indispensable
to the angler. They give him an
excuse for fishing and justify
the fly rod without which he
would be a mere vagrant.

Sparse Grey Hackle

Many of us probably would be
better fishermen if we did not spend
so much time watching and waiting
for the world to become perfect.

Norman Maclean, *A River Runs Through It*

After that first trout I was alone in there. But I didn't know it until later.

Richard Brautigan

I can catch catfish from dusk till dawn.

Hank Williams Jr

I take off early in
the morning, fishing
rod in tow, and
just drift about the
ocean all day.

Perry Como

Adopt the pace of nature:
her secret is patience.

Ralph Waldo Emerson

Patience is the art of
concealing your impatience.

Guy Kawasaki

Genius is nothing but a great
aptitude for patience.

Georges-Louis de Buffon

ONCE A FISHERMAN...

Once an angler,
always a fisherman.
If we cannot have
the best, we will take
the least, and fish for
minnows if nothing
better is to be had.

Theodore Gordon

For a man to admit to a distaste for
fishing would be like denouncing
mother-love and hating moonlight.

John Steinbeck

Even when I close my eyes
I'm thinking about it.

Rex Hunt on fishing

The curious thing about
fishing is you never want to
go home... you hate to leave in
case something might bite.

Gladys Taber

To the fisherman born there is
nothing so provoking of curiosity
as a fishing rod in a case.

Roland Pertwee, *The River God*

Poets talk about 'spots of time',
but it is really the fishermen
who experience eternity
compressed into a moment.

Norman Maclean, *A River Runs Through It*

I've gone fishing thousands of
times in my life, and I have never
once felt unlucky or poorly paid
for those hours on the water.

William G. Tapply

Of all the world's enjoyments
That ever valued were,
There's none of our employments
With fishing can compare.

Thomas Durfee

Fishing is much more than
fish. It is the great occasion
when we may return to the fine
simplicity of our forefathers.

Herbert Hoover

I love fishing. You put that line in the water and you don't know what's on the other end. Your imagination is under there.

Doug Larson

Most relaxing thing in my
life. It's therapy for me.

Deion Sanders on fishing

Oh, the gallant fisher's life,
It is the best of any.
'Tis full of pleasure, void of strife,
And 'tis beloved of many.

John Chalkhill

Go softly by
that river side
Or when you
would depart,
You'll find its every
winding tied;
And knotted
round your heart.

Rudyard Kipling, from 'The Prairie'

I suspect that so many of the
other concerns of men are
equally unimportant – and
not nearly so much fun.

Robert Traver on fishing

All good fishermen stay young
until they die, for fishing is the
only dream of youth that doth
not grow stale with age.

J. W. Muller